Easy Cooking for Tired People

By Y. I. Cooke

For Jessica and David

Contents

Easy Cooking for Tired People

My hours at work were increasing, my husband's cholesterol needed lowering. My tolerance for hot peppers and black pepper was non-existent. Michael Pollen's writing had warned me about the pervasiveness of low quality, pre-processed food at low priced restaurants.

Giving up eating was not an option. I realized that even simple cooking would be healthier than frozen dinners or takeout. It would be more affordable too. I stopped feeling apologetic for the simple fare and named it *Easy Cooking for Tired People.*

I could control for salt, pepper and sugar. Olive oil could be the main source of fat. Wheat could be whole wheat. Though I might only be producing a one course meal, with the option of fat free frozen yogurt or an apple for dessert, I could add elegant touches.

I used cloth napkins that dealt well with being unironed. A glass of wine at every home cooked dinner was far more affordable than in a restaurant. Since my kids were grown, candlelight was an easy option too. Sometimes I rinsed and sliced an organic lemon, removed the seeds and added it to our iced tap water. The idea was to have the graciousness that we had earned.

Week night meals took about half an hour to produce; on weekends I could take longer, but still wanted to minimize active prep time.

Generally, I made salads during the week with a base of pre-washed greens. I discovered that it was important to gently squeeze as much air as possible out of the bag before re-closing it. The goal was to keep the greens fresh over a period of days. On the weekends, I had more time to cut up and cook vegetables.

Grains, Potatoes, Root Vegetables

One way of injecting variety, was to vary the use of grains. They were all fairly easy to cook: measure the grain, measure the water. Bring the water to a full, rolling boil, add the grain, cover and reduce heat to a simmer. (Use leftover cooking liquid instead of some of the water; add a low sodium bouillon cube or a peeled clove of garlic if the rest of dinner was on the bland side.).

Potatoes and long cooking grains were for the weekend. Here are the proportions of 1 cup grain to cups of water and approximate cooking times. Start checking at least 10 minutes ahead of these times. Barley, brown and white rice, wild rice.

Grain	Water per cup of Grain	Approximate Minutes to Cook
Brown or White Rice	2	40-50
Wild Rice	3.5	60-90
Barley	2.5	60

Other grains were reserved for weekdays and hurried weekend cooking: Kasha, whole wheat couscous, bulgar and quinoa (pronounced *keen wah*). This was also when I'd serve specialty breads like pita and wraps.

Grain	Water per cup of Grain	Approximate Minutes to Cook
Bulgar	2	15-20
Couscous, preferably whole wheat	1.5	After grain is added to boiling water, cover, turn off heat and wait 10 minutes.
Kasha	2.25	20-25
Quinoa	2	15

I had two favorite ways for making potatoes without adding lots of fat. I could bake Russet Potatoes after washing the skins and rubbing them with olive oil. Depending on what else was in the oven, I'd give them an hour at 400° or 1-1/2 hours at 350°.

Alternatively, I would bake thin skinned potatoes of the Yukon Gold or red skinned type. After washing these, I cut them into bite-sized pieces. I put them in an oven-proof bowl or casserole, added 3 cloves of peeled garlic, and tossed them with about 2 tablespoons of olive oil. I covered them with a cover or tightly fitted aluminum foil and baked for 1-1/2 hours, at 350°.

This second method of baking potatoes works for other root vegetables too. For sweet potatoes, I peel them before cutting up. Instead of garlic, I add a pinch of ground clove and a few dashes of cinnamon. Any apple pie or pumpkin pie spices would work. It depends on what your family likes. The spices will bring out the sweetness in the sweet potatoes. Carrots work this way too and the pre-washed, pre-peeled baby carrots require the least effort.

If your tastes run to the earthy: Scrub and cut beets, peel and cut onions into chunks and wash and slice fennel bulbs. I don't add garlic or spices here, but it could be done. Toss with just enough olive oil to cover and bake.

Weekday Favorites

Chicken with Olives and Red Pepper

~~~~~~

Leftover Grain Salad

~~~~~~

Meat, vegetables and grain

~~~~~~

Pasta with Pesto

~~~~~~

Pasta with Sauce and Cheese

~~~~~~

Quinoa with stir fried vegetables

~~~~~~

Salmon Wraps and a word on sandwiches

~~~~~~

Shrimp with lemon and garlic

~~~~~~

Turkey Burgers

~~~~~~

Chicken with Olives and Peppers

This works best for 4 people or less.

At least one chicken cutlet (skinless, boneless chicken breast) per person
Olive oil to lightly coat frying pan (use a spray or rub a small amount on with your finger)
About 15 pitted olives
1-2 red bell peppers cut into bite-sized pieces
1 teaspoon dried oregano or basil
half a cup of white wine (or water)

Rinse Chicken Cutlets, trim off any fat or cartilage. Cut thick parts in half or even thirds horizontally. Keep them attached or not, but the idea is to have uniform thinness for quick cooking. You can avoid this horizontal cutting step if your supermarket has already done it.

Saute, over medium heat for at least 2 minutes on each side.

Add pepper, olives, oregano or basil, and white wine.

Cover, turn heat down. Simmer for 10 minutes.

I like this served with kasha and a green salad. Add sprouts to the salad if you like them.

Leftover Grain Salad

This is a chance to use up extra cooked grain.

cooked grain (about 1 cup per person)
1 - 15 oz. can of chickpeas for every 2 people
leftover cooked vegetables in bite-sized pieces
small pieces of:
tomato, pepper (fresh or roasted), cucumber, finely chopped celery, apple, pear, etc. (Whatever you have, whatever you like, whatever is in season)
chopped nuts or, for an elegant touch, about 1/2 tablespoon of pignolias (pine nuts) per person

Mix all ingredients.
Serve on a bed of lettuce, or salad greens, with dressing.

Meat, Vegetables and Grain

This is more an idea of getting everything needed into a one bowl meal than a specific recipe. Feel free to vary.

Chopped Beef (Hamburger Meat) – $\frac{1}{2}$ lb. Per person
Medium to Large onion
$\frac{1}{2}$ - 1 lb. Mushrooms
zucchini
small or large can of tomatoes (whole or chopped)

Brown the beef, in a frying pan, breaking it up as it cooks.

Peel and chop the onion.

Wash mushrooms. Remove woody pieces of stem. Cut each mushroom into 4 or 5 slices.

Rinse the zucchini. Cut it into bite-sized chunks.

Remove the beef to a bowl using a slatted spoon to minimize fat. Cover with a plate to keep warm.

Rinse the frying pan in very hot water to remove the fat that the beef left behind.

Saute the onions and mushrooms, over medium heat, stirring occasionally.

When the onions and mushrooms begin to brown or the onions look wholly translucent, stir in the zucchini.

Add the entire contents of the can of tomatoes and the beef.

Stir, cover and cook on low heat for 5 minutes.

Serve with grain; if you have leftover grain, reheat it in the microwave.

Pasta with Pesto

Serves 3

1 lb. Whole wheat pasta such as spirals
Prepared Pesto Sauce
2 - 5 oz. cans of tuna packed in water

Cook pasta in boiling water. With whole wheat pasta, I start testing for being done after 9 minutes. I find it more palatable as it softens.

Drain pasta and add pesto sauce to coat.
Break up tuna and toss with pasta.

That's the bare bones recipe, but often I use cut up smoked chicken breast (which is pre-cooked), or defrosted cooked shrimp instead of the tuna. Leftover chicken would work too. I occasionally use red pesto sauce, based on sun dried tomato, instead of green, basil-based, pesto. I have added halved cherry tomatoes to green pesto and leftover steamed asparagus to any kind of pesto.

Since this is a savory dish, I can add fruit to the green salad for a sweet contrast. This is more about thought than effort.

Pasta with Sauce and Cheese

Serves 3

This is comfort food with quality.

1 lb. whole wheat spaghetti
canned organic tomato sauce
grated cheese, can be part-skim, or fat free, mozzarella
or cholesterol free soy mozzarella

Boil the pasta for 9 minutes and start checking for softness.

Heat the sauce in a microwave safe bowl with a microwave safe cover, 1-2 minutes

Drain the pasta and pour on the sauce.

Serve the cheese with a small grater.

Green salad or steamed spinach would be a good accompaniment.

Quinoa with stir fried vegetables

The big idea here is that quinoa is a quick cooking grain, but it is also a complete protein. With vegetables, it is a complete meal.

quinoa ($\frac{3}{4}$ cup of dry grain per person)
olive oil to lightly coat frying pan (use a spray or rub a small amount on with your finger)
red Bell Pepper (anything, but green pepper which is less ripe and less sweet than other colors)
onion
mushrooms if you like them
zucchini or other thin skinned summer squash
asparagus, if in season
spinach

While the Quinoa is cooking per the instructions above, peel the onion, wash the other veggies and trim tough parts. Cut into bite-sized pieces.

Saute the vegetables over high heat, stirring frequently. Start with the vegetables that take longer to cook: Onion, mushroom, pepper. When those start to brown or the onions are translucent, add the quicker cooking veggies: zucchini, asparagus, spinach.

After the slower cooking veggies are stirred in, add a tablespoon of water, cover, turn down heat to low, simmer for 5 more minutes. Serve over the quinoa.

If you are feeling vitamin deprived, add a side salad.

Salmon Wraps and a word on Sandwiches

Serves 3

1 lb. smoked salmon (if you can get salmon trim, instead of slices this will be just as good, but less costly)
4-6 wraps
Cream Cheese (Regular, reduced fat, or cholesterol free soy or cashew)
Two large tomatoes sliced and/or
A jar of roasted red peppers, drained and cut in strips

Depending on the age and interests of the eaters, you can roll the wraps in the kitchen and cut into pieces or the wraps can be assembled to taste at the table.

A green salad rounds out the meal.

Though a meal of sandwiches and salad is simple, it is an opportunity to right one of the wrongs of restaurant eating. A high end restaurant will start your meal with a delicious basket of breads. One can forgo most of the bread or risk ruining one's appetite or one's waistline. However, on sandwich night at home, you can focus on a wonderful bread: Think roast beef on seeded rye or turkey breast on olive bread. It's the bread that lifts the sandwich out of the local 24 hour diner and into the realm of the gourmet. Shop accordingly.

A variant on this theme is a choice of 2-3 different breads, 3 different cheeses and cut up fruit or a garden salad. If one of the diners is a cholesterol watcher, add 1 or 2 varieties of hummus as a cheese substitute.

Shrimp with lemon and garlic

Serves 3-4

1lb. of large frozen shrimp (26-30 or less/pound), (peeled, de-veined, tail removed)
olive oil to cover pan
1 clove garlic
1 teaspoon dried oregano
1 lemon
a dash of white wine (or water)

Here's the hard part: Remember to defrost the shrimp in the refrigerator overnight.

Rinse the shrimp. Dry with paper towel.

Squeeze the garlic through a garlic press.

Saute the shrimp and garlic together, stirring frequently, until the shrimp is pink, about 3 minutes.

Stir in the oregano.

Squeeze in the juice of the lemon, but not the pits.

Add a dash of white wine.

Cover and cook on low heat until the shrimp is white inside. Test every minute or two, shrimp cooks quickly and is best not over-cooked.

Serve with a quick-cooking grain. Since shrimp isn't heavy, you might add grated, or thinly sliced cheese to your salad.

Turkey Burgers

2 quarter pound turkey burgers per adult eater
An equal number of whole wheat mini-pita
About 1 sliced tomato for every 4 burgers
Honey mustard (or ketchup)

This is a healthier burger with a healthier substitute for the empty calories of the average bun.

Broil the burgers for 14 minutes, flipping after 7 minutes. Serve each burger, on a split pita, with a slice of tomato and honey mustard or ketchup.

A green side salad completes the picture.

Weekend Favorites

Baked Chicken
〰〰〰〰〰〰

Baked Salmon
〰〰〰〰〰〰

Chicken Soup
〰〰〰〰〰〰

Roast Chicken
〰〰〰〰〰〰

Chicken and Broccoli
〰〰〰〰〰〰

Turkey Meat Loaf
〰〰〰〰〰〰

Baked Chicken

This is much easier to cook if you go to a store that sells kitchenware and get a basting bulb and a gravy strainer (which looks a bit like a measuring cup).

1-2 Chicken Quarters per person or the equivalent in chicken parts for the wing or drumstick lover
$\frac{1}{4}$ cup salad dressing per chicken or equivalent
$\frac{1}{2}$ cup orange juice per chicken

>Before going out for the day, put the chicken in a bowl, pour the salad dressing, then the OJ over the pieces trying to distribute it around.

>1-3/4 hours before dinner, preheat the oven to 350°; spread the chicken pieces in a single layer on a baking or roasting pan. Pour on marinating liquid (marinade) to cover. (You can line the pan(s) with aluminum foil to make clean up easier.)
>1-1/2 hours before dinner, put the chicken in the pre-heated oven.

>While the chicken is cooking, baste it every 15 minutes. This is important for juiciness. If there isn't enough liquid in the pan, add more marinade or even water.

>You can cook potatoes or vegetables too while the oven is on or a long cooking grain on the stove top. I particularly like wild rice or barley with chicken.

>After 1-1/2 hours, the chicken will be done. Pour the cooking juices into a gravy strainer. For the family, bring the gravy strainer to the table on a plate; for company, decant the juices into a small pitcher leaving the fat in the gravy strainer.

Baked Salmon

Serves 4

If the recipe is increased, don't put more than 1-3/4 lbs of fish in each package.

1-1/2 lbs of salmon fillet
1 medium tomato
4 scallions
1 zuccini
1 red pepper
white wine (optional)

Pre-heat oven to 400° for 15 minutes and remove salmon from refrigerator at the same time.

Wipe the salmon with a paper towel dampened with white wine or water.

Place the salmon on a piece of aluminum foil in which you can wrap it easily, think big. (The foil should be on a baking or roasting pan for ease of handling.).

Wash vegetables and cut in large pieces or slices.

Place vegetables on top of salmon fillet. Wrap everything tightly.

Bake for 30 minutes after the oven pre-heats.

Place package on a platter or plate. Unwrap and slide the fish and veggies onto the platter, a spatula may help.

Brown rice and a green salad are all that are needed to complete the meal.

Chicken Soup

What follows is a stove top recipe. However, the same ingredients can be cooked on low, in a slow cooker, for at least 7 hours.

3 skinless and boneless chicken thighs per person
2 big celery stalks per person
1/2 clove of garlic per person
a fistful of parsley per person
$\frac{1}{2}$ lb. carrots per person (to save a step, use peeled, baby carrots)
$\frac{1}{2}$ lb. thin skinned potatoes (e.g. Yukon Gold) per person

Place chicken thighs in a large pot with lid.

Rinse and trim any brown spots off the celery and cut in bite sized pieces. If you are using celery leaves, keep in large piece and remove after cooking. Add to pot.

Peel the garlic and add to pot.

Rinse parsley and add to pot

Peel carrots, trim, cut in chunks, add to pot.

Scrub potatoes and cut in chunks, add to pot.

Barely cover with water.

Bring to a boil over high heat. Then turn down to low heat. Simmer for an hour.

Remove garlic, parsley and any celery leaves.

This is a one dish meal, but would be even better with the crunch of a green salad and bread sticks.

Roast Chicken

Serves 3 people per Chicken

Approximately 3.5 lb. Chicken
3 Garlic cloves or a heaping teaspoon of Smoked Paprika
Orange Juice or water

Pre-heat oven to 450° and take chicken out of refrigerator immediately after.
Discard giblets and any clumps of fat that you can pull off the chicken. Place in an aluminum foil lined roasting pan.

If you are using garlic, peel 3 cloves and place in cavity of chicken.
If you are using smoked paprika place in small bowl. Add water gradually to form a paste. Using a spoon, rub the paste under the skin of the chicken breast.

Pour a small amount of orange juice over the chicken to wet the skin all over.

Place chicken in pre-heated oven. Immediately turn down temperature to 350°. After the first half hour, baste with juices every 15 minutes.   If there aren't enough juices to wet the chicken, add more orange juice or water.

The chicken should be done in 1-1/2 hours. (However, a larger chicken will take longer.) Let sit for 10-15 minutes before carving.

Since you are turning on the oven anyway, you can bake russet potatoes or sweet potatoes. For company, you can bake cut-up combinations of veggies.

Chicken with Broccoli

Serves 3-5

This is a quick dish to make, but the rice to go with it takes longer than my weekday meals. Start the rice, before you start prepping the chicken and broccoli.

1 skinless, boneless chicken breast per person.
1 bunch of broccoli for 3-5 people.
Red bell pepper (Optional)
1 medium garlic clove per person
1 tablespoon cornstarch
1 tablespoon dry sherry (or similar, e.g. medium sherry, dry vermouth)
1 tablespoon soy sauce (regular or reduced sodium)
4 tablespoons sesame oil

> Prepare the vegetables: wash the broccoli and bell pepper and peel the garlic. Cut the broccoli florets into small pieces, halves or quarters, including cutting through the attached pieces of stem. If you plan to use the thick, main stem, peel it and slice it very thin, (less than $\frac{1}{4}$ inch thick).
>
> If you are adding a bell pepper, remove the seeds and stem and cut into pieces about 1 inch square (exactness is unimportant).
>
> Chop the garlic finely or put through a garlic press. Set the vegetables aside.
>
> Slice the chicken breasts into the thinnest slices that you can manage. A sharp knife is important here. If any of the slices is more than 2 inches long, you can cut it in half for manageable eating.

Put the sliced chicken into a bowl and sprinkle on the cornstarch. Mix to coat the chicken. Add the sherry and soy sauce, mix again.

Heat half the sesame oil, in a big frying pan, over high heat. Add the vegetables and stir fry for 5 minutes. (Pretty constant stirring, but I listen to the radio.). Remove the vegetables with a big spoon to a plate or bowl.

Add the rest of the oil, add the chicken. Stir fry over high heat. After a few minutes, the chicken will turn white. Check, about once a minute to make sure one of the thicker slices is white all the way through. Add the vegetables back and stir for one more minute. Serve with additional soy sauce on the side and chop sticks for those who have mastered them.

Turkey Meat Loaf

Serves four hearty eaters.

2 lbs. *dark* ground turkey, 93% fat free
1 medium onion, chopped, or about ½ cup pre-chopped
(essential ingredient, do not omit)
olive oil
1 cup plain bread crumbs, preferably whole wheat and 1
teaspoon herbs (e.g. oregano) *OR* 1 cup flavored bread
crumbs
1 cup liquid (I have used tomato juice or V-8 juice or the
last of a jar of spaghetti sauce with water added or the
last of a bottle of ketchup with water added)

Preheat oven to 350 degrees.

Simmer onion in a little oil until wilted and translucent.
If it starts to brown, stop cooking immediately.

Using a fork, mix onion with all other ingredients in a
mixing bowl.

After mixing thoroughly, transfer to a loaf pan. I use
a pan with an insert that has holes at the bottom to
drain fat. Line bottom section of loaf pan with aluminum
foil for easier clean up. Just for the look of it, I draw
lines in the top of the loaf, with a fork, before baking.

Bake in pre-heated oven for 1-1/2 hours.
While the oven is on I often cook potatoes or carrots
too.

I turn the turkey loaf out onto one plate then turn it
onto a second plate to show off the fancy top.

Cold leftovers, if you have any, are very good.

Other Ideas

While the focus here is on simple home cooking, there is no reason not to get the occasional assist in the form of a beautiful loaf of bread or a rotisserie chicken. You can use your limited energy for the other elements of the meal.

A few foods are so good that they need very little cooking. When tomatoes are in season, I can eat them everyday; slicing is enough. I can stir fry asparagus, but plain steaming is less work and quite tasty. Quality steak is another easy choice.

There are also recipes, like beef stew and chicken soup that adapt well to a slow cooker. They are good for time shifting your cooking effort and coming home from a long day to the aroma of a good dinner. There are cookbooks that can be bought specializing in the slow cooker, though every slow cooker that I've owned has arrived with recipes.

My current favorite for my slow cooker is:

Chicken Cacciatore

Serves 4

1 16 oz. jar of Marinara Sauce
1 medium-large onion, cut in half and each half cut in slices
3 cloves of garlic, peeled, chopped fine or put through a garlic press
1 green bell pepper, washed, seeds and stem removed and cut into pieces about 1 inch square (exactness is unimportant).
8-12 <u>skinless</u>, <u>boneless</u> chicken thighs
6 ounces of mushrooms, washed, woody stems cut off, and quartered or buy them washed and pre-sliced in the supermarket.

2 tablespoons of white wine, if handy

Pour about half the tomato sauce into the slow cooker. Add the onion, garlic, pepper and chicken. Then add the mushrooms and white wine. Cover with the remaining marinara sauce.

Cover the slow cooker and cook on high for 3 hours or low for 6-7 hours. Serve with grain or pasta and a green salad.

For a varient:
Use plain tomato sauce. Substitute dried prunes or apricots and a dash of cinnamon for the garlic and bell pepper. Omit the mushrooms and wine.

Broccoli 4 ways

Besides chicken with broccoli, I have 4 ways of making broccoli as a side dish:

Steamed

~~~~~~~~~~

With Cheese

~~~~~~~~~~

Asian

~~~~~~~~~~

In Wine

~~~~~~~~~~

Broccoli should be fresh and not cooked to death.
Broccoli should be green, not yellow. After rinsing, cut the broccoli florets into small pieces, halves or quarters, including cutting through the attached pieces of stem.
If you plan to use the thick, main stem, peel it and slice it very thin, (less than $\frac{1}{4}$ inch thick).

Steamed

Steam broccoli for about 6 minutes. When you can pierce the stem easily, but before it turns olive green, it is done. Check frequently. Use leftovers in salad.

With Cheese

Add shredded cheddar cheese (fat free is fine) to a bowl of just steamed broccoli, stir to melt cheese.

Asian

Mix a tablespoon of rice wine vinegar and two tablespoons of toasted sesame oil and an optional teaspoon or two of ginger paste. Pour over a bowl of steamed broccoli, mix to coat. Good warm, cold or room temperature.

In Wine

(combination of stir fry and simmer.).

Results are not as pretty as in other recipes, but flavor is very good.

Heat $\frac{1}{4}$ cup of olive oil in a frying pan.

Add a clove of garlic which has been peeled and cut in half the long way. After the garlic starts to darken, remove it.

Add cut up broccoli to pan and stir to coat with oil.

Pour in about 1 cup white wine. Turn down heat and simmer about six minutes. Check stems for being easily pierced with fork.

Afterword

Since writing *Easy Cooking for Tired People,* I have had the good fortune to retire. I'm not quite as tired, but I still don't want to spend my life in the kitchen. There have been two main changes to my cooking:

- I've relocated to a place that is known for its fresh fish and seafood. This has added variety to my menus.
- Most nights I serve both a cooked vegetable and a salad. As a result, I've added my broccoli recipes to *Easy Cooking.*

Printed in Great Britain
by Amazon

32173838R00020